to cleave

Mary Burritt
Christiansen
Poetry Series

Mary Burritt Christiansen Poetry Series
Hilda Raz, Series Editor

The Mary Burritt Christiansen Poetry Series publishes two to four books a year that engage and give voice to the realities of living, working, and experiencing the West and the Border as places and as metaphors. The purpose of the series is to expand access to, and the audience for, quality poetry, both single volumes and anthologies, that can be used for general reading as well as in classrooms.

Also available in the Mary Burritt Christiansen Poetry Series:

The Music of Her Rivers: Poems by Renny Golden
After Party: Poems by Noah Blaustein
The News As Usual: Poems by Jon Kelly Yenser
Gather the Night: Poems by Katherine DiBella Seluja
The Handyman's Guide to End Times: Poems by Juan J. Morales
Rain Scald: Poems by Tacey M. Atsitty
A Song of Dismantling: Poems by Fernando Pérez
Critical Assembly: Poems of the Manhattan Project by John Canaday
Ground, Wind, This Body: Poems by Tina Carlson
MEAN/TIME: Poems by Grace Bauer

For additional titles in the Mary Burritt Christiansen Poetry Series, please visit unmpress.com.

to cleave
poems

BARBARA ROCKMAN

University of New Mexico Press | Albuquerque

ISBN 978-0-8263-6075-5 (paper)
ISBN 978-0-8263-6076-2 (electronic)

Library of Congress Cataloging-in-Publication data is on file with
  the Library of Congress.

Cover illustration: *Cloudburst, Ashokan Reservoir* by Kate McGloughlin
Author photograph by Jamie Clifford
Designed by Felicia Cedillos
Composed in Dante MT Std 11.5/13.5

For my husband, Rick

Contents

I

Snow Cave   3

Three Peaches on a White Plate   4

At Rest in Rain   5

Omen into Number   6

Absence of Wind   7

Flying Home from the Pacific Coast Rim,
    I Consider the Rio Grande Rift   8

In the Diner of a New Day   10

Even in Jungle Heat, a Red Leaf Falls   12

II

Note from Snow White to Rose Red   15

Red   16

In Dreams We Are All Things   17

The Coyote   18

My Maternal Grammar   19

Fragile Fabric I Might Be Made Of   20

III

Gulls of Loblolly Cove   23

While She Slept, Her Husband Made Chai   24

Letter from Georgia O'Keeffe to Alfred Stieglitz on
    Seeing His Photograph of Her Hands   25

My Husband Comes Home from Work   26

Love after Stalemate   27

What I Married Into   28

Gold Locket I Wear   29

Dream Ode to the Sleep of Long Ago   31

IV

Birthing Beach   35

News, Sendai, Japan | Beach Walk, Sanibel Island, USA   36

Testing Heaped Earth   39

My Daughter, Drowning   40

A Bridge Spans but Does Not Cradle   42

Island Sabbath   43

Sightings   44

V

My Hipster   47

Onto Her Tattooed Back, Bedtime Story I Tell My Daughter   48

The Raker Is Burning   50

Of the Coal Blue Field   51

The New Farmers   52

Ravens   53

Spring   54

Chamber Music   55

Reverie on the Frayed World   56

Our Names Are Many and a Mystery   57

Sisters Consider Repair   58

VI

The Assembled Discourse   61

To My Husband, Collector of Found Objects   62

Stranded in the New Age Bookstore   63

Traffic   64

Dear Husband from Afar | Dear Wife of a Thousand Years   66

Dear Landlocked from the Western Coast   70

VII

Unclutter	75
Post-Laryngoscopy, I Follow News of the Trapped Miners	76
Afterlife	77
After Birding at Cochiti Lake	78
Arterial Detachment: I Contemplate Dimming Sight	79
Western Tanager	80
Outdoor Reading	81
except light.	82
Elegy for Myself	83
Last Morning Blueberries	84
Acknowledgments	87
About the Author	91

I

Snow Cave ✓

There was the dream of a room
a glowing a windowless cave
in which a girl might live
the sun slung low
I was a burrowing creature
cap tied under my chin
cheeks their own hot planets
the sun hung low it was three it was four
snow creaked beneath my knees
sweat at my neck breath steamed
before dark before supper
before the call to come in

sun nudging its orange ball
between my knees half of me in
on all fours half of me out
a door a roof coming true
and walls curving up and I
did not stop to think am I happy
did not pause to hear an odd bird
I'd have a house at dusk
I'd have a home before dark

Three Peaches on a White Plate

beside the tulips,
whose fingers, fisted for days,
fly open in a sprawl of red-dappled,
double-jointed wrists
and flushed palms.
Their purple pistils,
velvet nibs with which
they will write themselves.

In ripening devotion,
the peaches swell.

At Rest in Rain

My looking deepens things and they come toward me to meet and be met.
—Rilke

Settled in pine duff and broken flagstone   a deer's breathing

grand ears rotate   regal neck
branched headdress nearly lost in shadow
knees hidden beneath chest and rump

> That he chose my small wood
> that I chose this moment to gaze

> from my house of plates and pages
> through a dark pane

His mate lowers herself   antlers confused with
piñon boughs   they turn in unison   their eyes widen

Hour of   *They laid themselves down*

> Later I might say to my husband   *if only you*
> or to a friend   *a sign*
> or to my sudden god   *Amen*

Omen into Number

Four sleek snake faces rise out of floorboards.
Four gold stalks erupt from a vase of snow.
Four made my family. In all directions
a separate question. At the four corners, dust swept up
in a glass shovel. At each quarter hour, arrows
nudged into niche and click. Rhythm
beneath rhythm. Four bulbs crack soil.
Four sons disband. Four seeds scored and soaking.
The day is divided into dawn, noon, dusk, and night,
and each of those is divided into grief, hunger,
inquiry, and relief. If snakes twine ankle and wrist,
will I wake to a wrong direction?
To whom do I say, I am trying to pray?

Absence of Wind

ruah: (Hebrew) Breath of God; wind

Windless dawn
               reties her sash   what has fallen remains fallen
     what has splintered will not be sutured

Windless noon
              tides recede   nothing strewn   nothing stolen
     a small room opens its door   one thought   two breaths

       What does a body do robbed of velocity?

       How does a throat bereft of *ruah* shape its plea?

Night
             star-becalmed and reluctant to speak
   a cry shudders dark grasses   bone cracks between teeth

     Give me the brow absent of doubt and need
     arms hung useless   sails collapsed

       In the trees   no rustle and bow
       In the field   no one flees   No disaster rising at sea

       Ruah: what quavers the throat's dark coil
       and returns to it   song

       Let fever lift
       May the pond rest unriffled
       May the blossoms be given one more day to be praised

Flying Home from the Pacific Coast Rim,
I Consider the Rio Grande Rift

The aerial view is shatter   web sprung   rung out

Alluvial fan cools the surface   freezes it varicose
cheeks wind-seared   thighs laced with dark ganglia—

a hewn place where suffering is long and
softening is brief

      not the misted coast
      not the wavering line of pelicans into which the laggard is welcomed
      nor the meadow of poppies tendering thin, orange cups

strata's slow reveal—
crimson   cardamom   and glare   repeat down canyon walls

      There is a pattern to my country
      to why I resist beauty's collapse
      why I seek *other than this*   suffering

is long and softening is brief

      not the deer bringing her young to high grass
      not her mate's furred antlers alert to incident
      nor the seals' heft slapped to rock

I return to malignancies   scarred mesa   reshuffling of silt
what was once ocean is fossil and drought

      Not torqued spruce whose roots clamp eroding bluff
      nor fog-dipped tides   crest and spit
      then   quieter   sequined

Of two countries   I

press one knee into damp pine duff

one into cold-pressed beach

dangle one leg over canyon rim
one curled in a heap of shards

settle into what opposition might teach

     it is eternal   it is brief
     blown poppies' whisper
     the hawk circles

I may or may not be home

In the Diner of a New Day

There are two mornings on the menu.
You can order the light fare
or the lumberjack.

With or without real time,
with or without fresh-
squeezed conversation.

The girl holding
her small pad, pen poised
and eyes down, is familiar,

and facing you in the booth
is a self you knew
to fail at courage.

The slick, fingerprinted menu,
smeared with token wisdoms
and bad breath, lies open.

And though you are ravenous
from a night of knee-breaking
hikes toward heaven, nothing

describes a plate that will
smell like the sack of clover
and lavender you'd hoped for,

nowhere is the beverage
that will coat the throat
with a stream's tumbling.

The morning of twin reckonings
is yoked oxen pulling
opposite directions,

is the quandary every maker
of lists and days faces,
territory of chefs and sinners.

You might plunge in, choose
from Morning A   Morning B
the way God must have.

Thorn-studded   Smooth-stalked
Garrulous   Silent
Swimmers   Walkers

Still, the shy waitress
on the checkered linoleum
waits at the foot of your unmade table,

its shredded napkins, its salt and pepper
lighthouses harboring an overcast day.
You cannot, for the life of pie cases

and *Today's Specials* embedded in black
corrugated signboards, conjure
an answer. You think

it helps to believe a story. You think
you might ask for the lunch menu.
And the waitress is so patient.

Even in Jungle Heat, a Red Leaf Falls

Last day's walk in paradise
I turned to my left, where I'd never looked.

On a log in dark foliage, a turkey vulture,
its robes dragged in dead leaves.
From the tip of its beak, a bead of water.

What does it mean that his eyes were dull coals,
that his hooked beak was that of an orthodox *rebbe*
descended from a tribe I come from, that he drooled,

that when he trudged arthritic into underbrush,
his knees cracked, dust fell from his moth-eaten coat,
and, I swear, he groaned?

I walked the day's slick body, saline blind,
breasts glued to thin cloth. Every yard, feverish;
every block overhung with lethal leaves.

When I rounded the last turn,
the brackish roadside canal. Twenty days
I'd recorded: crushed Coke, tinsel, unrolled *Volusia News*.

On its grass-matted lip, an egret,
as if opposition were the day's dare to see
the bright world: its legs, beams in the lightning field,

sibilant neck, *s* upon *s*—bird more air than night.
White trail I might slalom and sing, undulate. Do I overstate

that grace lit a route from grief?

II

Note from Snow White to Rose Red ✓

It was my job to keep them alive,
to feed and mulch, clip back dead growth,
to please mother.
How formal it seemed
what she hoped for,
one on each side of the walk.

When the dove became our pet,
when the fawn stayed
and then the bear,
I combed snow from his coat,
bottle-fed the deer, filled my hand with seed.

I never wanted to wander the woods or
clip that vile dwarf's beard free of the log.
I followed your adventure.
Never wanted the double princes or the castle or
for mother to stay on, uprooting, resettling roses.

Remember the tales I told you?
I wanted to stay curled under quilts,
but you seem pleased with your prince.
Mine is a distraction; I crave
forest paths, hare and stag.

Tell mother I'm sorry the roses shrivel.
Tell my prince he's no match for sisterhood.

Dear Red, my hand is still in yours.

In solitude,
Snow

Red √

My brother had a fire truck he pedaled furiously,

wide-nozzled hose and a gray bell.
I had a red plastic hat emblazoned
#2 and a red wool coat with brass buttons.

Back then I was a girl, cherry cheeked. I clanged no bells.
I sat on a kitchen stool and drew the robin's breast,
knew its curve and throb, its black claws, its green grass.

The breast requires shading, new Crayolas.
Red is the bird's heart about to burst.
Back then I was a girl, no pole to fly down or squad to name me,

but I knew how to toss a lobster into a boil.
I knew red-winged, cardinal, fever, flush.
If he had muscle to propel the engine, I had blood to stain the page.

I would weave my three-wheeler with vermillion ribbons,
quick-thumb my silver bell and scarlet the road
within an inch of his engine.

Somewhere in my future, women of crimson mouths
shook out a red dress, held the raspberry cords to the chariot.

Back then I was little sister, robin throb in my flat chest,
a scepter hidden in the lining of my brass-buttoned coat.

In Dreams We Are All Things

Their short, slim legs wrapped
around her sleek back,
a large black and tan dog paddles

the lake's perimeter through cattails
and water grass, carrying two children,
their faces untroubled, legs like loosed ribbons.

One body gliding—
the unblinking dog
focused on safe passage;

the miniature girl
clasps the dog's shoulders.

Every length of green growth
that slides against her thighs, pleasing.

The boy behind her hums,
dips and lifts his arms,
mimics the waving cattails.

Underwater, the dog's heart churns.
Underwater, the girl's flesh whitens,
her hands cup and release.

His pale back, lake jeweled.
Her shoulders, cloud furled.
The blue day sways behind them.

The Coyote

came close enough   the dogs
   were a racket of wanting
a bigger bite of wildness

Hunger slowed   the coyote slunk into rusting
   brush and we went inside craving
evidence   blood   stench   fur

certain I'd heard her teeth
   meet rabbit bone as we watched
night lit by the neighbor's porch

Back behind orange rectangles
   of glass   our songless talk
slippered feet   the tea kettle
   imitated nothing of tendon tear
its shrilling   no scar on the dark

All night the dry aspen scratched
   ancient text above our bed
all night his breath was creased notes
   pressed into my pillow and our dog's
musty huff filled the intervals
   of ticking   leaving nothing

but my heart's heft of wet apples
   memory of a red-kneed girl running
the length of a blank autumn field
   chasing a white ball   sweat
promise of something crisp
   and fallen to bite into

My Maternal Grammar ✓

is derived from decorum,
its formal syntax
spare and only
occasionally spontaneous.

Inherited mother tongue
of *simple but elegant*,
the Shaker chair,
Japanese arrangement,
chamber music, and

the classic line, matching
shoes, the understated
and asexual. At all costs,
curb vanity and her kin,

so life became the pursuit
of slang and cleavage,
Bohemian boudoir,
dark bars with dancing—

who cares so what
no one's watching bliss
I'd die to be fluent in.

Fragile Fabric I Might Be Made Of

It was as if each breath
had escaped a pouch
stitched *denial*.

Its threadbare silk
giving way, the way
I shook out
my grandmother's velvet gown,
and except for the seams
it crumbled to dust.

Dusk downpour
and the intersection
opened its black book.
One paragraph bled into the next.

At dawn, clawing leaves
under the dogwood,
my fingers hooked
a bird's withered chest.

I searched its sockets for pearls,
the intersection for a word,
tested velvet ash as a surface
to draw upon.

Only the skeleton
of dress loosed to breeze—
a frame I could enter.

III

Gulls of Loblolly Cove

are beak to beak,
no, beak in beak,
on kelp-clad rock.
Late afternoon
and their hunger
is not morning's
for live catch
dropped and split.
Rather, it is bird lust I witness.
How wide she had opened her sharp lips
and shrieked for him. Now, they
beak wrestle, thrust and twist as if
they had our tongues to tangle with.
I missed the exact moment
they released each other,
but he flew first,
east,
then she,
her polished yellow eyes
wild with indecision,
west.

While She Slept, Her Husband Made Chai

to cleave: *crack   splinter   stick fast to*

crushed cardamom   clove   peppercorn
it was for a purpose   mortar and pestle   his wrist
   scoop into black tea

not a man of kitchens   he smashed black star tips

late kitchen   dim kitchen
black kitchen she'd blunder
into walls   while he slept

   chai steeped

her hands held out as if it were her mother's
     spice brownies she wanted   mother and her
                spices on plastic spinners

all over the house flies settled   little clove flies
star cow   cloven child   how soft night was

clove darts into orange flesh
     that pleasure!   a whole
            language of the cloven
     the cleaved

Letter from Georgia O'Keeffe to Alfred Stieglitz on Seeing His Photograph of Her Hands

Be calm, Alfred. No,
I am a plain woman. I rinse dishes,
pull weeds, and unleash the dogs on dirt trails.
I sleep in a narrow bed. I rise early.
These are hands that mix paint,
decipher sky. With these hands
I scratch my head at the improbable.
I twist them under my breasts in sleep.
Fisted against my stomach they fly
from my body in dream. Hands
at the tips of wings, Alfred.
How you splayed my fingers,
insisted I caress the absent forelock,
empty sockets, each stone molar,
imagining the horse's rough tongue.
I want nothing of death, Alfred, nothing
of absence. These elegant hands cup seeds,
cut back echinacea, snip herbs for the sauce.
They tug knotted shirts from a basket, shake them
into light, clamp them to the line with bleached pins.
What can a man know of a woman's hands?

My Husband Comes Home From Work

Home, he heads straight for the dog,
hunches into her tail-thumping love.
I think, *One night I might find him*
curled in that bed of fart and fur.
But he straightens, lifts his eyes,
their concrete bottom and the dead
leaves trapped there. *Pile of shit,*
idiots, I was this close
this fucking close . . .
Stir-fry popping in its pan. He looks at me,
a furious, rumpled man,
Don't ask, don't even bother,
says, *I'm gonna take the dog out.*
Rice steams as I take out plates.
He returns, unclips the leash,
stares at his beer,
If I buy a year, I could retire in two.
But I hear, *If I lie here, I could fire a bear,*
and I see the hulk of infested fur
flattening him, its arms and claws
like tent lines pinning him to gravel.
He swallows, searches the deserted
hummingbird feeder, says,
I'm gonna change.

Love after Stalemate

First she thought   mind was the cabinet of answers
books would drop clues   lids would lift and spew
folded notes jittered with tiny lights
that would telegraph what was needed
to turn the stuttered axis   but it was not
the steps or koans or what others
had discovered of God

It was the cupboard of cups
thigh into groin   palm to neck
and the shelf of bowls   hips spilling accusation
It was tongues like bees caught in late-season blooms

Last ditch   her hollows like leaves beaming up from the stream bottom
while water wings sang   *dervish me divine*   There was no

practicing it or quoting   no posting to a thousand friends
no mention of charge   or balance   Tender tally
it was   off the table   taken up   which is to say
as with certain debt   they forgave

What I Married Into ✓

Salt into meat
browned briefly.

Carrots, paprika, potatoes.
As it is written on her greased page.

I sing *Dayenu*, improvise verses
as I churn the soup.

Bitter herbs, chopped apples, cinnamon.
Matzos wrapped in linen.

Silver goblet for the prophet.
Shank of a lineage I'd refused.

The woman who loved my husband
without doubt I bring to every choice

was certain her recipe would not fail,
the matzo ball would be light,

our daughters would marry well,
the brisket would be tender.

Mother-in-law of big bosom,
sequin and shocking pink,

took me in—hug
into faith I'd waited for.

Today, in my kitchen
littered with pots and peelings,

parsley limp in its strainer,
I want her bossing, her sass, soft arms,

her gold rings
in the dish by the sink.

Gold Locket I Wear ✓

Artisan of pawn raised on Manchester's
steel smoke and locomotion,
he folded his handkerchief,
strapped one valise shut,
went out from his land.
And though it was not his father's

fleeing the blazing *shtetl*,
no snapped candlesticks,
no pharaoh's terror, still
my grandfather
of the lovely hands

crossed the flannel sea,
the secondhand sky.
Freckled and folk song,
jewels sewn into his cuffs,
he was as likely as any to founder,

but he loved the iced deck,
the white-capped night,
gleam that rimmed each porthole,
brass bells, the idea of gold melting
coins into charms. Gripping the salt rail,

he did not know his hands
would unknot chains thin as thread,
that they would empty the watch
springs and gaskets on velvet,
that he would rub his palms

gently and get to work;
that what my grandmother
pinned to her chest,
what caressed her neck,
what held her auburn hair,

the boy's hands would grow into
this gold disk my fingers pry open,
photoless against my skin.

Dream Ode to the Sleep of Long Ago

I can't forget the dreamed girl's scratched face
or my dream dad out back chatting with smokers.

Wind witching wrappers, garbage cans tipped
downhill, dogs raving past midnight.

Haunted by that fast-scabbing girl, I am
insomniac minus father to ease me down.

I fear she might
revisit a next night. It would be easy

to be hurtled by a wind such as this,
forced like a last prayer into a wall chink.

Yet, I muse, *yet*, the dogs have it gnawed
down to the hollow. And still want more.

Oh, that I might be Daddy's beach girl again, share
his kite, his grin and sea chanties at my back,

sand-crusted and sunburnt,
hosed down, fed and fabled:

There you are, my salt-eyed pretzel,

not so bleary, not so unblessed, scarred
dream girl dismantled, and a story coming

on father's lips to please *Your Curliness—
off you go, hopping eddies. Every wind*

*has a dress she slips into, not a stitch too loose.
Down you go, dear miss.*

*Bees in the buttonholes,
berries round the hem.* So he begins . . .

IV

Birthing Beach √

Seal swept   I come   closer to be among crescents
want to be comma   to be paisley planted against   to be of the pattern   but
obey the STAY BACK signs   As tides slick those bodies   I want to be among
the young   A mother never stops arcing   her body half pond they come to

A cow bellows   black gush   the pup
clamps her heft   no shake-off   no peel-back
whiskered snout barnacled to rock   sides designed with scars
she has spent centuries swelling her thick hips

An orphan tries to latch   Mother after mother slaps her off

I am left with green wind
        and the seals moaning

News
Sendai, Japan

Horizon had not yet consulted shore,
nor the sand set its edge. Plates shifted.
Sea swept in. Windsor knots
centered. Bowls rinsed of rice.
Docks of crates. Admission of love.
Hello Kitty strapped to a girl's back.
Umbrellas tight as spears.

He has not found

his missing son   nor she
her wheelchair-bound mother

Family garden disappeared:

walls for leaning against, disappeared;
scythe in the shed, gone: shed, blade,
its need of sharpening.

Where was my house, asked the girl

new signs:

Beach Walk
Sanibel Island, USA

Grapefruit, bougainvillea,

whelk, coquina, scallop.
I return the live, pocket the
fractured.

Collectors drag their nets

LEASHED DOGS

playground closed
sealed windows.

                                        Open shutters, dolphins
                                        and the gulf's
                                        convulsions, petit mal,
                                        yet I scan
                                        the sand: there, my girl
                                        reapplies

sunblock.

                                        My hands could ring her
                                        waist:

helpless
the world. White masks,

kilometers of particles:
the reactor's rods boil
and spew.

At the edge,

                                        my husband, not missing.

Distant,

at the end of the pass

                                        he lifts binoculars.

                                        I practice my grip,
                                        his wrist. Later,

                                        tourists will toast

a fiery horizon,

                    but it is morning
                    in heaven

                    air soft as soot.

Testing Heaped Earth √

I lifted my gown. It was spring.
The yard trenched, and loam delivered.
Naked, I sniffed the composted

and combustible. Eyes closed
and arms wide, I fell the way a diver
swans. Small brown clouds puffed up

as my thighs sank into it,
breasts relieved of carrying.
I smelled what worms smell.

Fingers like cropped rakes.
Nipples, miniature trowels.
And hips tilling.

The neighbors
might have claimed
suicide by dirt, but hearing

dawn dogs start up, I pressed out of
the mess, blurred silhouette.
Loam strewn, went in.

Down the hall, dark leavings.
I might have made them breakfast,
might have mixed berries into batter.

My Daughter, Drowning

Clouds reflected in the kiddie pool covered her   submerged on her back
Her suit not hand-me-down   nor new   white fish on bleached blue

stretched over the little grave of
her belly   Wonder bubbles up   from the bottom

she was the snatched starfish I towel wrapped
pressed into black orchids   my breasts

and then stillness   and then the
out breath the opposite of

The clouds moved off as they do
so you wonder if they were

Her wet head   my spandex heart
Plastic chair slats stamping my flesh

and the suburban moms pretending not
staring into the burning bones and freckling shoulders they clenched

It was the clouds like bloated fish
that swallowed and then   lifted up my girl

There were no tears

It was August and her sister in the big pool   practicing the backstroke
Her arms longer than   which is why I recognized hers among the yards of them

The mothers' visors were white   Their knees dry
Seventy-three percent humidity   though the clouds had cleared
Later the eaves would overflow   Later
I filled bowls with luminous macaroni   their bickering

and then their dad home   picking at his tie on the edge of the bed
they jumped   their suits dry   breaking out the song
the smaller one always   singing louder

A Bridge Spans but Does Not Cradle

Rio Grande Gorge, remembering Isaiah

I will   his bone shatters
    winch   resuscitate
up the gorge rock
               river of water witch
       shrieks her children   fierce as Grimm
         there is no moral
feather weight   best boy
   scholared and raven scald   flying son
herald the wreckage: no, it is   chorusless
      those nested walls rockslid, yes
down   down the boy   his not yet gnarly hands
     his glued back brow   no limb   no claw grip: savior, no
the fall was swift   poor fevered fish
       and finless   was there one white feather?
: orphaned mother   : father become bent echo
     workless week of   wings
      he was a lovely specimen   of heft and capillaries
eyebrows and spleen   songs in his ear
         not written over
whirring found but
   did not rescue   did not rescue   found but, oh
   whistling heart   blue fledgling
oh, the rocked boy   gravel clattering
   tip of the down-filled cup   lip down   rib down   he was

Island Sabbath

Brevity, the week's text—

loons lapse into sweet redundancy

We take up an offering:

fern silhouettes and the dew-slid pines

We grow habitless
    fast from reading into things

: arc the rabbit leaves after leaping
: lake surface the loon zips tight and feeds beneath

Pre-dawn, bridge invisible in fog
we drive off island

unfolding our second skins
we exchange our currency

each gear, a violence   in the dark
we count our change

deny contraband:

   skipless stone   bird bone   mouse skull
   maple candy   our skin
                flushed with
                      observance

Sightings √

Did the bloated wren, claws curled to its breast,
attest to fate or ingested bait I'd spread
for grasshoppers? Every sign
my instinct to kill.

Even jays who drilled for berries at my screen
mistook glass for sky, collapsed
into the ice plant—blue feathers
like loose threads.

In a boulder's curve, a calliope.
Its humming heart frozen.

At dusk, a finch struck my headlight,
fell to asphalt. I drove on.

Through rush hour's crush, my daughter
willed a stunned pigeon, *Fly!*

Later, her thrilled song
from our flat roof
until I screamed, *Off!*

My girl's flapping arms
fell to her sides.

My Hipster ✓

wants her marrow to shine.

Once, scab-kneed and miraculous, she
flew her Schwinn downhill, looping potholes—
barrel racer of the cul-de-sac. Optimism
in neon leggings. Headstand and cartwheel,
witch and pirate. Till the bill of goods arrived.

She ripped its wrapping.

Then and there her insteps snapped,
hips slimmed to no womanly good.
She stilettos the runway, breastless,
famished. My urban blood and bone
is out till dawn, done up and done in
by two boys who compare her: *fuck you.*

She writes a poem on the train,
Desire is a vintage gown cut on the bias.

Every flaw riots a girl's good nature,
twists a waif's waist till it's knotted laundry
dragged down the alley of ice she slips on.

She is that beautiful,

thread of snivel coating her lips,
all her filthy stuff rumpling her like storm.
She counts stars, flat on her back in the *wish-I-might.*

Onto Her Tattooed Back, Bedtime Story I Tell My Daughter

Side of my hand crosshatches her back,
This is the plow breaking the field,

harrowing. When furrows are ridges a child could straddle—
planting, I say. My fingernails spray seed.

Will it be wheat, hay, or corn?
Hay, for the cows in winter, she says.

Palms pack earth—*tamping down.* Her grin
hidden in pillows. *Storm coming,* I say.

She presses into her sheets. *Lightning is a blazing whip.*
My fingertips dash and dive, her flesh ajitter with rain.

Cracking open, sprouting. She is
supposed to be drowsing, but we are giddy.

Seedlings rise amid daisies and black-eyed Susans.
Summer is ending, I say. *Oh,* she sighs.

Even at twelve, at twenty, her voice
the girl's at first telling. Birds and insects cross.

Almost fall. Harvesting. I mouth mowers trundling.
Knuckles trample tall grass.

My hands
are scythes sweeping hay. *Dusk,*

before dawn's baling—pack and lash;
my fists skid and brake. *There.*

Her breaths spaced where grass once waved.
It will rest a winter, maybe two. Fallow. Snow will cover it.

I blanket calligraphy at her waist,
the dove inked into one shoulder.

I don't say, *Cut flowers wither,*
a stricken mouse.

Leaving her dark room, *Sweet fields,*
I say, *sweet hay.*

The Raker Is Burning

A dozen piles I did not invite
my small daughters to jump or build rooms or imagine a house

Kitchen of dead umber   table of crimson
I raked the undone elms   shedding maples

Floor of paper   flame under stew   a locked door
For Sale tagged the house *over with*

Town of white pickets   stone walls I'd leave
dusk turning green to scarlet

My socks filled with bits of it
their picky habits   torn pages   I might

have fallen back into it   one hill of the village I'd made

sun puzzling through bare branches
                              I might have lit a match

Of the Coal Blue Field

At four, my daughter learned *coincidence*, renamed it
clinky dink; for years our defining of fate's collisions.
Ink in that word and rings round Saturn.

Last night the Mercury moon, sated sorcerer,
staggered out of the foothills. We see his slow stroll home
through a coal blue field and the street's oval glows
morphing into buds, snug in the leafing out, safe as the tucked-in child.

The writer at the glass podium said *seeing* is his subject
and *rendition* his obsession.

Venus, torched and steady.
Rabbit in the moon. Dog in the sun. I come full circle,

back to morning's red finch on the black mailbox,
belly like an apron of cornmeal edged with crimson
strings the monk scattered after blessing the house.

Reap and rapture. A day swings on its beam,
balances and scales back, hovers and falls.
Just so, the caught lesson,
sought-after news.

The New Farmers √

In suburban backyards,
past usual bark and holler,
there is bleat and cluck.

One of the new farmers bikes to work.
One has given up meat. They suffer
sore joints and burnt brows,

refuse daily news, tune the radio
to *all music all day*, read dusty
Whitman and Blake. And though

covenants forbid a rooster,
they invoke *don't ask, don't tell*,
raise chickens behind latched gates,

nudge eggs from fat females
who puff and doze,
and make of morning

a romance. One will go in,
kiss his partner's grizzled cheek,
whisk an omelet of chèvre and chives,

slice sun-warm tomatoes and bread
kneaded in the dark. Long ago they
learned to tame the hip, curb the kiss,

but this feast eaten from Adirondack chairs
facing sunrise, the misted hour, is a reprisal
of an old hymn to a land they refuse not to love,

country they dig their hands into
despite a litany of signs it will return
a spare and blemished harvest.

Ravens

Having clipped their nails
and clacked their castanets
from our flat roof, the ravens
have flown to black limbs
to practice imitations
of hooded highwaymen
and surly nuns. Who knows
what they're scheming behind sleek brows
and indented chests. To what dark rooms
do they remove? On whose
felt-covered table do they play
their hand? And what do they
make of white bags fraying
in their trees, streets colored
with crushed cans, and
cups' straws stabbed mid-suck?

They rise for trucks, veer
languid, resigned to cars.
Discuss camouflage
that women and men refuse—

                  rumbled cloud, bramble, drift,

costumes that resemble lift
and flocked freedom ravens live—

                  aerial vantage, pocked canyon, plunge.

The ravens slap their tambourines.
They want to be surprised,

                          see our bodies rise.

Spring

Every shoot and blade saying,
Now, notice me now—yellow tulips
open so wide it seems their petaled arms
will break behind while arriving plums
flaunt their best-of-show pose—my daughter,
at three, counts *blossom trees* as we drive,
numbers beyond what she knows but
wanting to name delicate explosions.
How she loves the plosive word.
Blowing her lips and popping
tongue to teeth, *Blossom*, she cries,
blossom, her whole mouth becoming
the thing she loves.

Chamber Music

Twice this summer the thrashers
produced young in the nest
under the porch eaves, and twice
the fledglings fled.

As the cellist melds
with two violins,
I am folded
into space,

opened
by two daughters,
twice departed,
and wonder what thrashers do

between broods,
what music their world
offers—wind, downshift,
howl or buzz—
how, through loss,
we renew ourselves.

Reverie on the Frayed World

Moths gnaw hung fabric as I sleep.
Shaken into morning, the once tight-knit is
chapel of collapsed glass, windows grilled
with what thin fibers sag and sway.

open weave   unravel   give way

When my small daughter studied the roiled clouds
and spied a snatch of blue at their center, she said,
God's room. Daily, I walk a reckoning
with what prayer and poem can do.

break   realign   split

I never taught my daughters to mend,
backstitch, hem. Is it too late
to thread a needle, snip a patch,
hum them toward how a world heals?

knot   repair   render whole

In the shop of scissors and patterns
I study tiered spools, lineated dawn to night.
Heaps of looped yarn, a hundred heathered tones.

I choose remnants to fill bitten space,
address my daughters' awkward hands:
Consider shrink and give. Leave extra thread.

We steady the needle's eye,
enter failed fiber,
suture the impossible,
exhale.

Our Names Are Many and a Mystery ✓

When the apricot tree blackened, we cut it down,
readying to fill its hole with memory, but

fresh shoots sprouted, and next season bore foreign fruit,
the tree rechristened *peach*.

I suppose we are grafted from mixed ancestry,
that unimagined histories live in us.

Within us, darker skin or lighter, hair less coarse or
straighter, hunger for a diet of meat or spice we swear

we've never tasted, sudden faith in scripture
we've never read, and our tongues shaping

romance, guttural, dream linguistics never practiced,
then, an urge to draw a bow, to plow,

an itch to roam frigid terrain or tropics
we've not traveled but call us home.

Who can name what sap moves through us or
what weather renews us,

but that dead tree rose, and tugged too soon,
refused to release new fruit.

It clutched its second coming as any of us given
another chance at living.

Sisters Consider Repair

They'd straddled apple trees as girls
knew the whiff of powder pink
        the tight bud   the sister business

        licking each others' scraped knees   pins twisted through lobes
        peeling back scabs   filthy fists knock-knocking the other's chest

        Once when they'd dared to fly off the flat roof
        the first landed and caught the younger

        But they no longer   climbed and fell

They crafted a tale

                In turns they'd suck the other's demons
                Older's bitter swallowed by the younger
                The younger's doubt gulped by her sibling

One would bite down
and leech from her sister's flesh
comings and drownings

The other would twist the blistered burn
into a gut-thin pouch   fifth breast
she'd glue   between two chests

        Just so   replenish   and compress distance

VI

The Assembled Discourse

Blade enters fruit   juice covets it
Keys rise   a pianist presses down
The heron tips its underwing   light fills it

Opposition ferries us shore to shore
Night on one continent   dawn on another

She eats meat   he shivers
He harvests   she lies in a furrow of thorns
He reaches   she reverses and this
omits unrecorded innuendo

For each resolution   table of crumpled documents
and a floor spiked with broken pens
We inch toward tolerance   yet
force the raft into back current

Like this   we marry
We spit slogans   split chores   declare heresy
believing we know what concord means
Our sources muddied   snagged by cattails
we slog the opposite bank

When women proclaim   men whisper
Table tugged apart   gaping   we add leaves
The surface appears   seamless
Clean paper anchors each place
Dissenters slouch and snicker

When one tips back to yawn
the other scratches a new doctrine
Floor on which their chairs scrape

To My Husband, Collector of Found Objects

Artist of assemblage,
I will trade some of what I covet—
rusted bottle cap, dead bees, chipped cat's eye—
for the promise of a daily prize pressed into my palm.

When I present sheaths of words, keep your red pen
pocketed. I lose accolades as others lose keys. I am at a sinking age.
Erase the gawk of lost tact. Revel me, not Once, but Now.

When my witch broom torches you,
remove my daggered hat; cajole the cackler.
Ease my body down. Tongue each rivulet and marsh.

I am famished for a Whitman's sampler. Ribbon me
with clichés in downturn and orange alert
through sweet breath and sour,

honey in the larder, chard on the plate,
from one eclipse to bitterest dark;
that is how to love me.

Stranded in the New Age Bookstore

In the hum of machine-softened air,
copper bells fill space where
negative energy might infiltrate.
Birds perch in a fenced alcove,
and walls are lined with texts
of Tao and I Ching.

The sign by the door says,
"It's bad karma to steal," but I did,
in the coffee shop where
stacked flyers for classes
conflicted with mine,
so I write on the back
because I have no paper.

No surprise
my keys are locked in the car.
I'm stranded in contemplation,
my aura so tainted
pure souls who slouch
in soft chairs and read
look up and know
I am in great need.

But the salesgirl beams with goodwill,
"He'll be here soon," meaning not the Messiah,
but my husband, whose day I'll be blamed for dismantling.

On the counter, fairies hold glass orbs.
I roll egg-shaped stones from the river in India
the cashier can't name, though she tries to describe
their power: *balance, protection, peace
of mind*, he thinks, which, surprisingly, I feel
moving out into a mild winter day,
staring down into my car where
the star wand, purchased here
by the man who is now lost,
holds my keys.

Traffic

Jumbled on my dashboard, a dozen ducks:
pirate duck, glitter duck, blue duck,
horned demon duck, so when
I braked they flew into my lap.

Though the piano tuner was deceived
and slid his card under my wiper,
Seems you have them all in a row: call me,
I resisted. It was laughable

that I had anything lined up.
The car clock froze years ago.
I had a delayed sense of it—
who I would be at the next light.

My mind, call minus response,
crushed metronome.
My heart, a missed turn.
Since I was a mother,

I thought balance of control
and chaos were what was meant
by future, yet it was never time
to weigh the heap of rubber ducks

scooped from my daughter's lap as
the latest accident spun past, never
time to estimate the heft of bags
under my eyes. Always,

the sugary after-school left my
fingers too slick to grip anything.
How could I know, when she
was hip-hop and tragedy,

that my daughter was archiving my
tuneless sing-along, veined hands,
wannabe lingo in a ledger:
Never, Never.

Maybe I would call him.
His fingers would be delicate;
his timing, his pitch, perfect.

Dear Husband from Afar ✓   Dear Wife of a Thousand Years

Dear Husband from Afar   Par Avion

I am abashed. I'd prefer this missive discursive, not listed, but
there is the getting through, getting right to.

Enclosed, please find a slim page, width of my smallest finger on which I have
transcribed in cursive with a fine-tipped quill Cruelties Committed in Marriage.
Upon opening the aero envelope, out will fall a miniature page that
hitting the floor will curl into a tight scroll the way a spider furls to hide
and shelter. You will flick or toothpick wide what will resist: my list,
which requires not forgiveness. With thumb pressure, unwind.
Spread tight, it reminds you of my wrongs. It is my confessional,
my chagrin, my humbling. This is bumbling preface to the mission.

A Public List: Missive of My Misdoings

> 1) frequent eye rolling, which interprets you unworthy
> 2) the hurry-up my hands do to urge you to your tale's climax
> 3) refusal to face you full frontal esp. upon arrival as, Oh, he's home, ho hum
> 4) countless, the turnings from your touch in the lair we share: I recoil
> 5) practice of interruption
> 6) omission of affection
> 7) deletion of praise

This is Phase One: *uno, un*, mere shred of what might further this endeavor:
rebuttal is expected. I ask you, am I a liar of the long marriage?
pretender to ardor? hypocrite of love?

You likely have a list to ensue. If this diction seems archaic, florid, distant,
not consensual, it is all I can flourish to disengage from long love's fallacy.
To face the plain and painful, I pursue it through an altered tenor.

Husband of multiple decades, I promise nothing, know not my intention
or my capacity for retention, *tenir*; in French, I learned the tenses. In marriage,
I need a lesson. I am a mess of nerves, worry that what retains us—house,
health insurance, daughters grown, the dogless rooms—is fiction.

This wound scroll, flimsy, thin, and winged, weighs less than what I conjure
our current love, and yet, from its rent fabric, a thread might stitch us a fresh sleeve;
not undo, but do us: a button at its cuff and so,

In Hope,
Adieu

Dear Wife of a Thousand Years ✓

Last night the Dodgers took a lousy loss, 9–0, to the Red Birds whose uniforms you love but I do not. I'm an LA fan through and through and you just like their tight butts, hand signals you always say are about other than strategy but it wasn't just the game but the roofer who didn't show and four hours overtime which made me miss the pre-game and leftover pizza that put me in a foul mood.

I'm sleeping with the same stuffed dog that watched you birth our first girl because we have no live and huffing mutt which we need to discuss because though you think I'm not ready to replace the dog who survived the Great Hurricane and you called Buddha of All Dogs, I'm lonely and it's not replacement but renewal. And by the way, I'm not renewing the *New Yorker*. The *Times* is enough for my week.

What is this Shakespearean lavish marriage chat? I think we're okay. I love you and it's great you're off writing in the jungle haze. Hey, have you seen the egret? ibis? a hawk? That river is famed for night creatures and burrowers which, I admit, I'm not but I think I'll clean my closet this weekend and you'll be surprised.

Don't worry so much about the List of Wrongdoings. Speaking of night creatures, how are you sleeping? Bet you love that you can turn the light on and write and read and think your middle of the night "who'd ever put all this on one page?" sort of thoughts which is probably when you penned that little missive which made me smile because I never thought I'd married a poet which you weren't and I did. Now I get to meet some amazing folks.

Keep your fingers crossed the Sox make it to the series. Remember the year your Dad and I drove across Massachusetts last minute to get to the play-offs? That might be about my best memory of Herb. He's probably where your love of writing came from if that sort of thing is inherited.

That little scroll is cool. It makes me think I should get into my box of found stuff and make something, a collage of broken things, which by the way we're not, *broken* that is. Maybe rusted, a little frayed, but it's nothing we can't piece together. There's a show by that assemblage artist up north the week you get back. Want to go?

I miss you, mistress of the long-winded reverie. How about that? *Reverie.* And I liked the "button at the cuff" touch. You must have buttoned those little cuff buttons for eight months after my stroke. I was embarrassed.

I love you way more than I love the Dodgers,
Your Hub of a Thousand Years

Dear Landlocked from the Western Coast

Waving grasses your eyes   mist deciphers
what we do and do not walk into

Weeks we watched rabbits leap in lust   one bounced to lure the other
poised paws   twitch & burn   speedy breeders

It is my habit   to step back   not toward
Our bumbling feet reverse rooms

Ocean is my call   and you not hearing
I am raucous harbor   and you   buoy and wharf:

>   I have seen neither seal nor cormorant
>   a dearth of deer this year   quail in hiding
>
>   One hummingbird surprised   despite brisk air
>   the moon eclipsed in multiples of three
>
>   I imagine you walked out   not coastal bluff but high-desert street
>   Did our red-eyed shepherd follow?

As if fern printed   as if splayed feathers pressed and glazed
beach is etched for reflection

If you were here I'd not name but nod toward
what we share

At 2 a.m.   I tug shutters seamless
drop detritus on a page

our different zones   common home
you   my lonely & lasting

I who clawed for distance
grow kinder hands

Soon
more fully ours

VII

Unclutter

Within their invisible hoop, shorebirds
angle and tilt like flung plates,

huddle to tidal streams, lift and orbit
as we, hooded against rain,

explore the floor of earth's house,
sucked into the moan of it—

we retreat to tide pools. Starfish
clamp bellies to backs.

Anemones exhale silver,
mauve, cling and swell.

Feet crack barnacled rock
as mussels hiss, tighten their grip.

Ruddy, gaping, over surf
and bird racket, through mist,

Look! There! we dissolve,
reappear breathless.

I name what I clutch to my chest—
gull wood, thumbnail shell,
half-dollar, claw.

He offers one purple spiral,
and, to receive, I release
my collection to beach and tide—

his cold hand,
mine closing over it.

Post-Laryngoscopy, I Follow News of the Trapped Miners

Passages collapse. Some take decades to fail. Seven
miles of tunnel one man ran daily, then sang,
shirtless, sulfurous, *Love me tender*. I was ice-

packed, feared nails had shut my airways.
Each man entered a tube and was taken up:
thirty-three lives predicted, *Never again normal*.

Fluttering in my ear as if a dozen bats wanted out.
The miners were blindfolded against brilliance.

I felt the collar that checks a dog's lurch.
Sutureless, I dreamt *Larynx insouciant* stamped on my report.
The tallest buildings are lower than the depths these men fed against.

What had been encrypted was lifted from my vallecula:
there is a dock between epiglottis and tongue.
We learn words as we need them—emergent,

they scratched their names. Men of the fist to the table,
daughter swung and set down gently. My inconvenience
was not cancer but, *put under*,

a soul worries. A swallow winged up grit, and my diction
shattered. We choose to sing or cringe in pain's company.
We rest on whom we never knew as the beloved.

Yet, quickly, we lose the tenderness fear gave us, the bell to ask
back on the shelf. I wanted to see what the scope saw.
The miners wanted to get laid, then drink alone.

I should have stayed breakable.

Afterlife

My husband sleeps in our long-gone
daughter's bed because he is
sick with the common cough
and breathing is tough   I have the big bed
to spread in and write and tonight
I love him   One day
things will get serious
We will be forced from each other's
common living   Dead we will
rendezvous   one bed   books
pushed aside to make room
his head clear and my hands
free of paper and pen
and what is
said will be all.

After Birding at Cochiti Lake

He comes home naming birds, eyes lit
with morning sky and wind off the lake.

All day, avian vocabulary
moves between us, and when

we roll close at night, I hear wings.
A junco twines a nest in my hair.

Across my back, a blue heron steps.
Tips of feathers brush thigh

and neck. A pintail duck paddles
beneath salt cedar through bosque

between us. My palms smooth
the sequined mallard. Silt slides from

our fingers. A rise of mountain bluebirds.
Rush of air, bald eagle lifting from pine.

Geese cry, reach the apex of sky, disappear
as we, in our unfeathered flesh,
drop down to sleep.

Arterial Detachment: I Contemplate Dimming Sight

The eye doctor shows me my fired orbs in 3-D:
moon corneas, sclera-flecked
lakes on distant stars.

A loose-knit cape thrown
over the earth of my iris
hides arterial debris.

Macular perplexity means
rely on the peripheral. He says,
Less life than expected.

Who knows what thrives on erupting suns?
What instruction resides in lesions
that lead the traveler toward heaven?

Soon, I will peel plastic shielding vision,
test the next intersection:

Goddess of blinding snow and
black ice I cannot see to brake for,
bring amazements. Guide me

to the hidden lake
where memory replaces sight.
Teach me the thousand ways to see.

Western Tanager

For days the town's aglow with yellow flight.
Red-knotted bolts of silk
limb to power line.

All I want is one crimson-crowned canary.
Twelve friends post the Radiant One on timelines,
but I have not been visited.

Thrashers carry foot-long sticks to eaves,
eyes the golden hue I seek—
coins tossed at my feet.

May 26, 8:16 a.m.,
swift as lightning's scribble
he crosses me: arrow feathered in tropical foliage.

Who'd expect his lemon zip line to snap-retract
before I cross the street, this blood-tipped knife
to graze my chest?

Outdoor Reading

I can pretend it will always be
this riffle of lime-green light,
trees unleashed,
end-of-day *hallelujahs*,
loose-wristed *praise-the-lords*.

How nice and cruel of you to ask,
the frail man will say
to the lovely girl leaning into him.

I can pretend the madrones' blotched
bark is not the man's cheeks, that I
do not envy the girl's smooth skin,

that I do not drift from the famous poet
beyond our folded chairs to a girl
gathering acorns—how I arranged
congregations into moss and singing.

except light. ∿

Pain almost stops me,
but captured by the warm fall yard,
I photograph corroded café chairs,
their peeling loops a découpage of shaped shadow.

A bee claws the aster's eye.
Aspens turn over aspects of amber
and shade, while sage lifts crimson lips,
even as frost derails its arch and beckon.

Because my unnamed illness
suddenly flares, the bright cup of rose tea
on the round iron table becomes a lens to remember
appetite, even as I hunger for nothing

Elegy for Myself

I have given up on being
beautiful, on debt, and detriment
to the ones I never loved enough.
The food was only fair most days,
the weather lacking, and the sex
not what I anticipated. Good-bye
climate of contempt, culture of claws.
I was not meant to live this long,
never memorized the code or
mastered the inflection. My thumbs not
fast enough. Good-bye tremble
and blush, spoiled pears, raw fish,
keys and petrol, paint samples and
drawers. Toss my crumpled pages.
Ink bleeds; there's no hereafter. *Finito.*
Adieu, fury, thorns, books, half-eaten orange.
Good-bye my anthills, gold ring, socks.
If there's another go round,
reconstitute me bold,
less lonely. Sift me
into the lake I love.

Last Morning Blueberries √

Knowing that these musty beauties
are the last to ring in the pail
that rinsed in the dented colander
and sorted
will tumble
into the white bowl
you will decide cream or not
sugar or not and
on which back step
to settle in sun or shade.
You will talk to the dog kindly
glimpse the goldfinch
lift the spoon
your teeth breaking into
such bitter such sweet.

Acknowledgments

These poems previously appeared in the following journals and anthologies:

Adobe Walls Journal: "The Coyote" and "In the Diner of a New Day"
All We Can Hold: A Collection of Poetry on Motherhood (Sage Hill Press): "My Daughter, Drowning"
Bellingham Review: "In Dreams We Are All Things" and "My Maternal Grammar"
bosque, the journal: "Love after Stalemate" and "Red"
Cimarron Review: "The New Farmers"
Compass Rose: "except light."
Ekphrasis: "Chamber Music"
Fixed and Free Anthology: "After Birding at Cochiti Lake," "Island Sabbath," and "Traffic"
Forge: "News, Sendai, Japan | Beach Walk, Sanibel Island, USA"
Jewish Journal: "What I Married Into"
Louisville Review: "Letter from Georgia O'Keeffe to Alfred Stieglitz on Seeing His Photograph of Her Hands"
Manzano Mountain Review: "Reverie on the Frayed World"
Modcloth Anthology: "Fragile Fabric I Might Be Made Of"
The Mom Egg: "Sightings"
Naugatuck River Review: "Onto Her Tattooed Back, Bedtime Story I Tell My Daughter"
Nimrod International Journal: "Post-Laryngoscopy, I Follow News of the Trapped Miners"
The Pinch: "Last Morning Blueberries"
Persimmon Tree: "Gold Locket I Wear"
Quill and Parchment: "To My Husband, Collector of Found Objects"
Santa Fe Literary Review: "Testing Heaped Earth" and "Of the Coal Blue Field"
Sin Fronteras/Writers Without Borders: "Stranded in the New Age Bookstore"
Shadow and Light Literary Anthology (Monadnock Writers' Group Publication): "Outdoor Reading"

Taos International Journal of Literature and Art: "Elegy for Myself" and "Birthing Beach"

Terrain.org: "Three Peaches on a White Plate"

Thrush: "Absence of Wind" and "While She Slept, Her Husband Made Chai"

Vocabula: "Ravens"

WomenArtsQuarterly: "My Hipster" and "My Husband Comes Home from Work"

———

I am grateful for the support and inspiration of friends, family, and fellow writers.

For the women who hold me, my Flamingos, Jayne Benjulian, Sandra Hunter, Marcia Meier, Tania Pryputniewicz, Lisa Rizzo, Ruth Thompson, Michel Wing, and Barbara Yoder, words will never express my appreciation and amazed good fortune.

Kyce Bello and Ginger Legato, fierce and blessed sisterhood, thank you for wisdom, belief, best advice, and poems that astound me.

For the group that reads and offers fresh vision, Deborah Casillas, Robyn Hunt, Donald Levering, Anne Haven McDonnell, Gary Worth Moody, Mary Morris, and Kim Parko, I am lucky to be in such gifted company.

Leonora Smith and Julie Hampton, who hung the poems on the walls of the ACA Library and imagined this manuscript into being, bless you!

To my mentors, who enliven my work and remind me how to live as a writer, Marie Howe, Carole Maso, and Erin Belieu, thank you for widening the path.

I am ever indebted to the good humor and generosity of my students.

Thank you to Rick, Beth and Elana, and David and Marita Glodt, family who buoy me with their belief and love.

For gifts of time, natural beauty, and inspired company, I thank Atlantic Center for the Arts and Playa Residency Program.

To the ever-passionate Kate McGloughlin for sharing her painting, "Cloudburst, Ashokan Reservoir," as the cover for this book, my deepest gratitude.

I am most grateful to the University of New Mexico Press, especially to Hilda Raz for the invitation to be part of the Mary Burritt Christiansen Poetry Series and to Elise McHugh for her unfailing optimism and support in ushering *to cleave* into being.

About the Author

Barbara Rockman is the author of *Sting and Nest,* winner of the New Mexico–Arizona Book Award and the National Press Women Book Prize. Her poems have received Pushcart Prize nominations, the Southwest Writers Prize, the New Mexico Discovery Award, the Baskerville Poetry Prize, the *MacGuffin* Poets Hunt Award, and the *Persimmon Tree* Prize. Her work appears in numerous journals and anthologies including *Bellingham Review, bosque, Calyx, Louisville Review, Nimrod International Journal, Taos International Journal of Art and Literature,* and *terrain.org.*

Barbara teaches poetry and memoir at Santa Fe Community College and in private workshops. She is the workshop director for Wingspan Poetry Project, bringing poetry to victims of domestic violence, and the poetry coordinator for inside] out Arts, developing poems with people living with mental illness.

A grateful recipient of residencies at Atlantic Center for the Arts and the Playa Residency Program, Barbara earned her MFA in Writing at Vermont College of Fine Arts.

Born and raised in western Massachusetts, Barbara Rockman lives in Santa Fe, New Mexico.